WORKING DOGS

WORKING DOGS

by George S. Fichter

A FIRST BOOK
FRANKLIN WATTS | NEW YORK | LONDON | 1979

Cover photograph courtesy of:
Grant Heilman Photography.

Photographs courtesy of: Evelyn M. Shafer: pp. 3,
8, 9, 11, 14, 44; Paulus Leeser: p. 17; U.S. Coast
Guard: p. 18; United Press International: pp. 22,
30, 32, 36, 39, 51, 54 (top and bottom); U.S. Army
News Features: p. 25; American Humane Association: p. 40; Miami-Metro Department of Publicity
and Tourism: p. 48; Smithsonian Institution, National Air and Space Museum: p. 58.

Library of Congress Cataloging in Publication Data

Fichter, George S
    Working dogs.

    (A First book)
    Bibliography: p.
    Includes index.
    SUMMARY: Describes the selection, training, and
accomplishments of various breeds of working dogs.
    1. Working dogs—Juvenile literature. [1.
Working dogs. 2. Dogs] I. Title.
SF428.2.F53   636.7'3   78–11345
ISBN 0–531–02887–9

Contents

WORKING DOGS

1
Dogs: Willing Workers

The roots of our companionship with dogs plumb time beyond recorded history. In those early times people lived by hunting. Wild animals were their source of food, and their only weapons were rocks held in their hands. Large animals were formidable foes, and survival was at stake with every encounter.

It was in these days that people formed their first bond with an animal—the wild dog. The two hunted together, shared in the bounty, and gave each other comfort and protection. Over the centuries, this close relationship has persisted and become even stronger. For most dogs, of course, their days as hunters are long in the past and the majority earn their keep today solely as pets or companions. Others still perform services that add to our pleasure or well-being. No other animals, in fact, have been used in as many ways as dogs have.

Dogs have fared well. Never in their thousands of years of association with people have they been better fed, given more comfortable living quarters, or kept in finer health. Nor in all history have there been more dogs—about one for every eight persons. Keeping dogs (and other pets) is a symbol of prosperity. Where getting food enough to feed people is a problem, pets are not common and may even be illegal.

Today, most dogs live longer than ever before and they share many of the diseases of our overpopulated civilization. For most dogs, their role today is almost exclusively to give and to receive affection. And they are indeed devoted friends, their loyalty unmatched by any other animal associates. They are stabilizers, preventing loneliness and filling a companionship void with purpose and appreciation. They teach young people responsibility, giving them an understanding of dependency.

Dogs demonstrate their devotion by risking their own lives to save the lives of people—often people they do not even know. Every year one particular dog is singled out to get deserved publicity and a financial reward for saving a person's life. In records kept over the past 25 years, the lives of more than 250 people have been saved by these heroic dogs. Among the recent dogs rewarded were: Meatball, a German shepherd (Alsatian) who protected his mistress by chasing away a burglar; Zorro, also a German shepherd, who rescued his master from an 85-foot (26-m) fall in a ravine; Skippy, a mixed breed, who saved

**English sheepdog
and puppies**

a six-year-old from a rattlesnake; Budweiser, a Saint Bernard, credited with rescuing two girls from a burning house; Tom, a Great Dane, who saved one child from a speeding car and, in the same year, saved another from drowning—the list is long and astounding. It is perfect testimony that almost all dogs like people and also a good reason why almost all people like dogs.

Most dogs do indeed thrive on serving people in some manner, either performing a definite chore or simply being friends and companions. This craving for love and approval is so strong that nursing pups may desert their mother temporarily to get human affection. Some dogs adapt so remarkably to their masters' ways that they acquire to some degree similar mannerisms and dispositions. A dog also learns words, or at least the tone or inflection that goes with them, so that it obeys commands and shows understanding. An alert and intelligent dog will even anticipate what is expected by its master's attitude and movements so that words are not even necessary. It is this willingness to serve that gave the dog its "best friend" reputation.

More than a thousand breeds of dogs have been developed over the years. Only about two hundred are recognized today by the various kennel clubs and dog associations in different countries. Only these dogs, with papers to prove their purebred ancestry, can be entered in the different shows and exhibits to win recognition and acclaim for their breed.

Nearly all dog organizations divide the breeds of dogs into half a dozen categories: sporting, hound, working, terrier, toy, and nonsporting. Several dozen breeds were developed especially to perform some particular kind of work, such as guarding, shepherding, or carrying loads, and even though for many this kind of work is no longer needed, the breeds are maintained. Dogs not belonging to the working breed category are sometimes workers, too, working hard for their masters to accomplish particular chores or to earn money. And many dogs with mixed ancestry—the mongrels or "mutts"—are also good workers and are as lovable, capable, and devoted to their tasks as are the aristocrats.

2
Keepers of
Herds and Flocks

From hunting, people turned to planting crops and to keeping flocks of sheep and herds of cattle. Dogs could do little to help with the planting and harvesting, but they were put to work immediately as shepherds and drovers.

Over the centuries, breeds were developed with special talents for this kind of work. Many dog specialists say these are the wisest of all dogs.

Herding dogs could do work that one person alone or even several could not possibly do. They kept the flocks and herds together and moved them from one location to another as their masters directed. They protected the animals from wolves and other marauding wild beasts—and also from human thieves.

Good dogs could be trusted to take care of their charges for days or even weeks all alone, while their masters went for supplies or were on other essential trips. All the dogs required was a cache of food.

(6)

Shepherds became so convinced that their personal dogs were the best and most skilled that they pitted them against those of other owners in contests. Working trials of this sort are still held to demonstrate the capabilities of these remarkable dogs in the handling of sheep and cattle. The dogs do their work rapidly and accurately, bringing the animals precisely into the pen or whatever position their masters command. Some of the commands are given by voice or by whistles; others are cues by hand. Once they size up the situation, well-trained dogs know automatically what is expected of them and can do their work without commands.

THE BREEDS

In Europe, almost every country developed its own special breeds for herding. Few of these breeds are still working today. Most familiar are the German shepherd (Alsatian), of Germany, and the collie, from Britain. Both have long since distinguished themselves in many other ways. Another famous breed from Germany is the schnauzer, and Britain is known also for the diminutive Shetland sheepdog from the Shetland Islands and for the shaggy-faced, almost bearlike Old English sheepdog.

Three breeds appeared in Belgium—the Groenendael and the Tervuren, both with long hair, and the Malinois, with short hair. Famous sheep dogs of France are the Beauceron, Briard, Languedoc sheepdog, Picardy sheepdog, Pyrenean sheepdog, and Savoy sheepdog; of Italy, Bergamaschi Herder, Macelbio Herder, and Maremma. Hungary boasts the big white and woolly Komondor and the smaller Puli. The Soviet Union's best known sheep dog is the huge Owtcharki, much slower than the smaller breeds but commanding because of its size and superb qualities as a guard.

(7)

Border collie

A Shetland sheepdog rounds up the flock.

Some breeds, like the German shepherd, were versatile enough to be used with either sheep or cattle. The larger dogs were preferred for cattle, however, and some were developed specially for this work. Among these are the Rottweiler, of Germany, and the Bouvier des Flandres, a French-Belgian dog. All, of course, have since been used in other ways, too.

Probably the most famous of the sheep dogs still earning its keep at its trade today is the border collie, which was developed in the hilly sheep country on the border between England and Scotland. It has since been spread around the world. These dogs are as fast as the wind and incredibly intelligent. They may even climb onto the backs of sheep to keep themselves visible and in a commanding position when the sheep are moving through a small area in a compact group. Many are used today in western United States and also in Australia and New Zealand. There they have been mixed with the native dingo, a wild dog, to produce the Australian Cattle Dog and the Australian Kelpie.

"EYE" AND "STYLE"

Good sheep dogs have both "eye" and "style." The style allows the dog to approach a flock without scaring them. The dog moves in a crouched position rather than rushing and causing the sheep to scatter. When the dog is close, its "eye" comes into play, for a good dog can stare so intently at the sheep that they are literally hypnotized and will not move.

Great Pyrenees

Part of this is natural, but an equal share is the ability of these clever dogs to learn. Some seem to do one chore better than another. They may excel at driving the sheep but are not as good at holding them, or vice versa. Shepherds may keep one or several of each, making dogs "heel" until it is their turn to work. Other dogs do both jobs equally well.

Welsh corgis, both the long-tailed Cardigan and the short-tailed Pembroke, are cattle dogs. Unusual for cattle dogs, they have very short legs and long bodies, almost like dachshunds. They make cattle move by nipping at their heels, and they escape kicks by ducking low.

Oddly, these dogs were first used to drive cattle away rather than keeping them together or on a particular trail. Before the lands were fenced, cattle wandered into the farmers' fields regularly and either trampled or ate the crops. To protect their fields, the farmers trained the corgis to dash off and chase away the trespassing cattle. The corgis were guided by whistled signals.

Corgis can also be trained to herd cattle, however, and they do an excellent job.

3

Sled Dogs of the North Country

An Arctic twilight becomes blackened by a blizzard, the snow driven by a howling 100-mile-per-hour (161-km-per-hour) wind. The temperature is −40° F (−40° C).

Through this darkness and bitter cold, a dog team pulls a sled toward an outpost cabin. The lead dog moves on a compass-precision course, the other dogs and the driver following blindly. Alone, the driver would probably have wandered aimlessly in the frigid wasteland, but he knows that the lead dog has an extraordinary sense of direction.

Soon the driver and the dog team have made it to safety. Inside the cabin, the driver is snug and warm. Outside, still in their harnesses and waiting for the storm's letup, the dogs are curled in the snow banked on the cabin's leeward side.

Pulling sleds or carrying packs, these dogs of the Arctic made it possible to explore, travel, and live in this land of ice and snow. The dogs have carried supplies, mail, and even people.

(13)

LOADS AND SPEED

Harnessed to their sled, each dog can haul about 50 pounds (22 kg) for distances of 20 or even 30 miles (32 to 48 km) a day. To show off their strength, dogs have pulled individually half a ton or more of weight, but this is not practical, of course. As many as two dozen dogs may be hooked to a sled, but usually there are fewer. Where the terrain is smooth, they can maintain a speed of 15 miles (24 km) per hour for hour after hour, and they do this on a sparse diet. Most drivers feed their dogs once a day, but others give them a meal only every two days. They are convinced that the dogs have more energy and work harder when their stomachs are not stuffed.

The dogs follow only word commands, for no reins are attached to their harnesses. The dog in front is the leader and makes certain the others are kept aware of this dominance. Now and then one of the team may try to loaf a bit, not pulling as hard as the others. The shirking may be so slight that the driver does not notice it. But the dogs in harness know. At the end of the day, they all turn on the loafer with growls, snarls, and bites—and the next day that dog pulls as hard as the others.

HITCHING

Sled dogs are most commonly gang hitched: that is, one dog in front and those behind him in pairs. They can also be hitched one after the other, or in tandem. If the load is light, the dogs cooperative, and the driver skilled, they can be fan hitched—

Siberian huskies

each attached individually to the sled so they form a single broad line or arch in front of it.

DRIVERS SELDOM RIDE

Contrary to common belief, drivers almost never ride on their sled, unless it is empty or the travel is downhill. If the snow is deep and loose, the driver often goes ahead of the dogs to help break the trail. If they are moving speedily, the driver generally trots alongside with one hand on the sled to help keep it steady. And to urge the dogs onward the driver does yell "Mush!"

For very fast travel, a person may ride on skis while holding onto the traces and letting the dogs pull. Without a heavy sled and with such an easily pulled load, the dogs can maintain a speed of 20 miles per hour (32 km per hour) for long periods.

SLED DOG BREEDS

All sled dogs grow thick, heavy coats that protect them from the cold. Their woolly undercoats are oily, shedding even icy water. All are muscular, none weighing less than 60 pounds (27 kg) and the largest weighing as much as 100 pounds (45 kg). Their big feet have thick, furred pads.

Four breeds of dogs were known in the Arctic lands. Once it was feared that the pure stock of these dogs had been lost, for explorers and adventurers going into the region took in other dogs to crossbreed with the Arctic dogs. They hoped to develop faster dogs, for sled racing had become much in vogue. But fortunately, enough of the purebred dogs remained in remote areas to preserve the breeds. All probably had the same ancestry, dating to the time when North America and Siberia were linked by the Bering Straits.

Jason, a Samoyed

**These sled dogs are resting
after a long haul in the Arctic Circle.**

The Siberian husky and the Samoyed developed on the Siberian side, the Eskimo dog and the Alaskan malamute in North America. All of the dogs are lovable and affectionate and they make good pets.

All four breeds are handsomely imposing, typically with a grizzled coat. Some wear dark "caps" and either "spectacles" or a "mask" over their soft, wolflike eyes. The most beautiful of the four is the Samoyed, which has a thick white coat, a heavy mane, and a well-feathered tail carried in a curl over its back. The Samoyed's black lips give it a seemingly perpetual smile.

TO THE NORTH POLE—
ONE MAN
AND HIS DOGS

On May 1, 1978, Japanese explorer Naomi Uemura became the first person to travel alone to the North Pole. Alone? Not really, because a team of nineteen dogs took him there.

Uemura began his 57-day, 500-mile (805-km) trek in early March from Cape Edward on Ellesmere Island in Canada and would have arrived much earlier except for unexpected problems along the way—blinding blizzards, ice floes that broke the connection to the polar ice cap and necessitated a wait for a freeze, and a marauding polar bear that ate all of his provisions, which had to be replaced. Midway in the journey, too, one of the sled dogs gave birth to six puppies. The considerate Uemura played midwife, then delayed his journey until a plane arrived to fly the mother and her newborn back to civilization.

4
Defending
Their Countries

Dogs began their role as warriors in ancient times. At first they probably served primarily to protect their masters as individuals. Then they became warriors themselves in battles of clan against clan and country against country.

The Gauls equipped their war dogs with a formidable array of spikes and knives that added to the animals' natural weaponry of teeth. The Romans trained dogs as fighters from puppyhood and turned them loose against the enemy in hordes—hundreds or thousands in growling, gnashing packs. In more than one instance it was these dogs that decided the outcome of an encounter. Dogs were still being used in attacking packs during the days of Napoleon and in the Spanish conquests.

In more recent times, dogs have been employed to a much more limited degree as actual fighters, but their usefulness in other ways in warfare has increased steadily.

DOGS OF
WORLD WAR I AND II

It was World War I that put dogs in challenging new roles in warfare. They worked as guards at prison camps, around munition storage areas, and at critical supply stations on the home front. Others served as messengers and proved themselves to be remarkably uncanny in making their way through enemy lines undetected. Still others were sent out to find the wounded, to carry medicine or supplies, and to act as scouts or sentries in detecting the enemy. Special schools were established for training dogs, and an estimated eighty thousand were in military service by the end of World War I. By World War II, roughly four times as many dogs had been trained by the Americans, English, Germans, Russians, and others.

Rin Tin Tin, one of the best known dogs of all times, was born in a German trench and abandoned there when the Germans evacuated before the advancing armies of the Allies in World War I. An American soldier discovered the puppy and took him home to the United States. There he was trained first as a police dog but later became most famous as a movie star. Rin Tin Tin not only made the German shepherd (called Alsatian in Britain) one of the most popular dogs in America but also established the notion that virtually no other breeds of dogs were used in war. This, of course, was not true.

Among the other kinds of dogs used in World Wars I and II were Doberman pinschers, Airedales, Saint Bernards, schnauzers, griffons, Belgian sheepdogs, boxers, and collies. In cold countries, Alaskan malamutes, Samoyeds, and Siberian huskies worked for the military as sled dogs. Retrievers and Newfoundlands served those moving in watery country and helped rescue

**Dogs are trained to aid
soldiers in the battlefield.**

drowning people. Dachshunds, terriers, spaniels, and other little dogs were also enlisted. One of their specialties was finding buried mines, sniffing them out with great accuracy and then sitting beside their find until someone came to remove the mine. This was especially important when the enemy began encasing their explosives in plastic that did not trigger the conventional mine detectors.

Only about half a dozen of these breeds are working for the military service today. Most versatile and outstanding of them all were the German shepherds, known for their intelligence and their responsiveness to training. Nearly all of the dogs in the K-9 Corps are German shepherds.

TRAINING IN THE
K-9 CORPS

In military service dogs get not only intensive training but also superior care—excellent food, a daily grooming, regular medical inspections, and great amounts of love and appreciation when jobs are well performed. Dogs are unique among animals in being satisfied with praising words when they do as commanded. Likewise, they can be scolded, a reprimanding voice "whipping" them more severely than a physical blow.

All of the dogs in the K-9 Corps first go through a basic training in which they learn the fundamentals of how to behave. Not until they respond without fail to such commands as No, Heel, Sit, Stay, Come, Crawl, Up, and others are they ready for special training to become a sentry, guard, or patrol dog. The dogs must learn also to get along with the other dogs in the K-9 Corps without quarreling. During this time, too, a deep and enduring comradeship is nurtured between dog and master.

Some dogs flunk out. Unable to take the training, they are discharged—or at least demoted to lesser responsibilities. Others show superior qualities. The best of these are singled out and bred to produce offspring that are equally exceptional. This selection goes on for litter after litter. The dogs in the K-9 Corps are becoming unquestionably the geniuses of the dog world.

The K-9 Corps wants more dogs with the bravery, devotion, and know-how of Chips, Pal, Bobo, Peefka, and others that achieved fame in World War II. These dogs earned special medals for performing unbelievable feats, such as finding and destroying by themselves entire machine-gun emplacements or attacking sneak patrols and snipers who could otherwise have caused great losses. Some of these dogs died in action and were buried in a special cemetery for dogs of war. Others were mustered out of service as hero veterans and took up a calm "civilian" life.

IN SOUTHEAST ASIA
More than a thousand dogs served with the American military forces in Southeast Asia in the 1960s. There they led patrols and kept on constant alert for possible ambushes. With their sensitive noses, they sought out booby traps, and at a command from their masters, they would attack and kill.

Military police use the dog "Yank" as part of a law enforcement team.

Confounded by these well-trained dogs, the enemy had shipments of cats brought in and turned loose in the battle zones, hoping the cats would distract the dogs. But K-9 dogs have a devotion to duty that not even a cat can divert. The dogs became so feared, as they were also by the Japanese in World War II, that often they became the primary targets rather than the soldiers.

BACK TO
CIVILIAN LIFE

The dogs were taught also to sniff out drugs that soldiers returning to the United States were trying to smuggle out with them. Some of these specialists continued in narcotic work in domestic service. But like the dogs of World War II, most of the canine war veterans were returned to civilian life.

First they were carefully rehabilitated to assure that they were ready to live at peace with the world and as friends of all people. This demilitarization is just as intensive as their training for war. It includes repeated tests, such as having people make menacing motions as they jump at the dogs from dark corners, riding past or around them on bicycles, and being subjected to the noise of gunfire and other commotions.

People who acquire these veteran dogs also get a record of what the dog did for its country while in military service.

5
On With The Show!

Precisely when dogs got into show business is not known, but we can guess how it happened. It is likely that someone taught a dog to do a few tricks and then began showing off the pet's talents to friends. When there came a perfect combination of an exceptionally intelligent dog and a sensitive, skilled trainer, the results were phenomenal. A business was born.

People would travel long distances to see the performance, or the trainer would take the "act" from town to town. Soon other animals were added to these shows. Some were trained, others simply exhibited in cages. But in carnivals, circuses, and vaudeville, dogs were always among the stars.

MOVIE STARS
When show business shifted to the movies, the dependable dogs continued to get big billing. In New York, Hollywood, and other cities of the entertainment industry, literally hundreds of dogs

(27)

are put through training paces every day while their trainers wait for them to be called. Each hopes to have the right dog for whatever part becomes available.

For dogs, the start in movies came in the late 1800s—at the very beginning of the celluloid industry. Most of the dogs got brief and secondary roles—as character actors, so to speak. But some became highly paid stars. Of all the movie dogs from past to present, Rin Tin Tin ranks as the greatest. This fabulous German shepherd (Alsatian) earned more than four hundred dollars per week, a fantastic sum in the 1920s, and achieved worldwide fame. When a poll was taken in 1925, Rin Tin Tin ranked as the most popular movie star in America. He made a total of forty movies before his death.

Because her audiences were expanded by television as well as movies, Lassie was seen by countless millions. Lassie—the original Lassie was a dog named Pal bought for ten dollars, but several other dogs played the Lassie role over the years—made the collie a most popular pet. Skippy, a wirehaired fox terrier, starred as Asta in *The Thin Man* series in the 1930s, and in 1947, Skippy's grandson inherited the role. The first British technicolor film featured a dog called Scruffy, and in the BBC's popular "The Forsyte Saga," Garry, a pedigreed collie, played the part of Balthazar, a dog that in the book was a mongrel.

Rin Tin Tin, Lassie, and other show dogs were so skilled and so popular with audiences that they commanded almost all of the attention in the scenes in which they appeared. To protect their own fame and popularity, some human actors flatly refused to work in movies or shows featuring dogs. They resented being upstaged by the dogs and having people go away remembering the dogs but not them.

BEHIND THE SCENES

Behind every dog actor and always off camera is a trainer who gives the dog its cues. It is these talented people who deserve the credit for making the dogs appear to be so intelligent and to understand the situations being depicted in the movie. The trainers could not be successful, of course, if the dogs were not cooperative, and the dog actors must also be "hams" when they are given an opportunity to show off. It is good teamwork that earns the pay and the applause.

All sorts of deceptions can be employed in movies. The audience sees only the final product—a skillfully edited version of all the pictures that are taken. For example, a dog races across the screen to save someone from disaster, such as a raging fire, a torrent of water, or perhaps even another attacking animal or hostile humans. The audience first sees the plight, then the racing dog—and the switching back and forth goes on, building into a tense drama in which hearts pound. Encouraging shouts and cheers come from the spectators as they live every second of the episode. These are climactic moments—and superlative entertainment. They are why an admission fee was paid to see the show.

But to get this effect, the dog may have been racing in response to a trainer's voice for some rewarding morsel of food. The dog's mad rushes can be filmed again and again and with a variety of obstacles. Finally the director is satisfied that enough pictures have been taken, and this footage is then cut and spliced into the disaster shots.

Actually, the disaster pictures and the dog pictures may sometimes be filmed miles and months apart, but in the final film, the two are put together in a way that captures the most

exciting moments of each. They appear to be one unit, and the audiences are awed by the dog's deeds.

Pity the poor pet pooch who gets chastised for not being able to match the sort of trickery that is possible with technology.

WHICH BREEDS MAKE THE BEST ACTORS?

Professional animal trainers keep a variety of dogs ready to answer calls. Some of the dogs are purebred; others are mongrels, or mutts. The trainers select individual dogs that seem to have natural show-off tendencies and then cultivate them. Some are more responsive than others, more trustworthy in front of an audience or in filming situations, or more anxious to please their masters, but with proper training, virtually any kind of dog can become a performer. German shepherds, collies, poodles—these are breeds demonstrating high intelligence and responsiveness to training, but if the part calls for a Great Dane, a Saint Bernard, a mongrel, or some other breed, the trainer cannot sign a contract unless he has exactly the kind wanted.

Comparing the level of training of these show dogs to humans, the dogs have advanced beyond basic college to a graduate degree. Few of the common pet dogs ever get the equivalent of a high school education. Rarely are they given an opportunity to develop their talents.

Trained dogs are popular with audiences all over the world.

"Benji" (right) and "Sandy" (left) join
the human star of <u>Annie</u>, Andrea McArdle.

CARTOON CHARACTERS

In the movie world, what real dogs cannot do is managed with ease by those in cartoons. Dalmatians became familiar to most people for the first time as a result of Walt Disney's *101 Dalmatians*. Disney's charming and nondescript Pluto endeared muttish hounds to almost everyone. These cartoon characters are so effectively personified that the carry-over to people's attitudes toward their own pets is tremendous.

LIVE PERFORMANCES

Dogs do very well in personal appearances. In live shows on television or on stage, they go through a repertoire of acts that duplicates what has been delighting audiences for centuries. Costumed dogs walk on their hind legs—or on their front legs. They stand on their head, balance on one paw, roll over and over like barrels going downhill, dance to music alone or with other dogs, climb ladders, and swing on trapezes. Their acts range from pure comedy to feats that are seemingly impossible.

Recently a dog charmed theater audiences by playing the role of Sandy in the popular *Annie*, a dramatic production that played to sellout crowds in New York and then in road shows that took Sandy to London as well as to major cities throughout the United States. Sandy was a mongrel rescued from a dog pound in Connecticut, and he not only escaped death but was soon catapulted to fame.

Like other dogs, Sandy entertained because he was intelligent and easily trained—and also because it is a dog's nature to please its master. There are people, however, who disapprove of this use of dogs. But most people enjoy seeing animals perform tricks.

6

"Eyes" for the Blind; "Ears" for the Deaf

In England during the mid-1960s, newspapers reported an unusual story about a dog leading the blind.

News? Yes, because in this case the blind was another dog. Its "eyes" belonged to a German shepherd, an old friend and companion.

When the German shepherd saw its friend failing and having difficulty finding its way, it voluntarily took up the chore of watching over the spaniel's needs and serving as its guide. Most remarkable, the German shepherd was not a professional or "trained" guide dog. It had taught itself. Holding the spaniel's ear gently in its mouth, the big German shepherd led its blind friend to food and made certain it got up and down stairs safely. It opened doors for the spaniel, and on a regular schedule, it took the spaniel on exercising walks in a nearby park. Yes, this was indeed an astonishing story.

As surprising, however, is the fact that in the thousands of years that people and dogs have been companions, the use of dogs as "eyes" for the blind did not come about until recent times. In the 1700s, a hospital in Paris provided blind people with dogs to help them make their way safely through the streets, but the idea did not catch on in a really big way until after World War I. It was the Germans who first began training dogs in large numbers as guides for blinded veterans. By the early 1930s, there were training schools also in the United States, England, and at least a dozen other countries around the world.

German shepherds are the most familiar of the dogs employed as guides for the blind, but collies, boxers, Labrador retrievers, and several other breeds have been trained successfully. And it is not only the dog that must be trained. The blind person who is to become the dog's master must also go to a special school, the two learning to understand each other perfectly. Between them there develops a love and a harmony of motion that makes them work as though they were one. The result is unbelievable, sometimes almost uncanny.

TRAINING THE DOGS

First the dog is trained. In one of the several schools that specialize in providing guide dogs for the blind, each potential guide dog goes through intensive schooling. This lasts for two months or longer. Although each dog is selected as carefully as possible before it is accepted, some do not make it to graduation, for the course is not easy.

Dogs are about a year old, mature but still quite young, when they are accepted for training. Each must demonstrate an

eagerness to learn and must be anxious to please. The basic training takes the guide dog through simple obedience exercises—the kind of training that all well-behaved dogs should have. These include obeying such commands as Sit, Stay, Come, Lie Down, and others. After these are mastered, the dog must learn to walk in a straight line just to the left and only a few steps ahead of the instructor or trainer. The natural inclination to stop here and there to sniff or to give attention to people, dogs, or objects are all discouraged with sharp reprimands. Praise comes only when the course is kept straight and without regard for what might disrupt an untrained dog.

HIGHER EDUCATION

In the next phase, the dog is put into the special harness that it will wear when at work. In the typical rig, a stiff U-shaped handle rises from the harness to hand-level height. From this time on, the dog knows that wearing this special harness means "duty." At all other times it can be a normal dog, but the handle is the touch communication between the dog and its master when the dog is at work as a guide.

Now the dog must learn to go forward when commanded and also to make right or left turns. It must also stop on command and then make no move until another command is given. Other decisions are left entirely to the dog. If a curb is encountered,

**Because of her guide dog
and the mobility he gives her,
this blind girl can go to college.**

for example, the dog must indicate to the instructor that they should stop—even insisting if the instructor attempts to go ahead anyway.

The dog must also be able to judge whether the space ahead is wide enough or high enough for its human companion to pass through or whether it would be better for them to go around. All of these situations are simulated in the school's training center, but as soon as the dog has shown a mastery of the school's course, it is taken outside the training grounds into real-life situations for a test.

When the dog passes this phase of training, it is taught to work in traffic. It must learn to recognize and to respect automobiles, trucks, and other moving vehicles. If the dog is given the command to move forward and a vehicle is approaching, it must disobey the command. But it can proceed if the vehicle is not moving. Every conceivable kind of traffic situation is duplicated in the school, and then the dog is taken into real traffic conditions for the final test.

TRAINING THE DOG'S MASTER

After the dog has graduated from training, it is ready to meet its real master—a blind person who has applied to the school for a guide dog. Often the blind person has waited for a considerable length of time, for there are always more applicants than there are dogs available. All applicants are checked carefully to make certain they are suitable, in physical condition and also in attitude, to work with a dog. The blind person must want the kind of independence the dog will make possible and must also be extremely fond of dogs. Only a small percentage of the applicants are accepted.

**While training with their guide dogs,
these two blind people met and later married.**

The training for masters consists of a month or longer of living with and learning the dog that is to become their "eyes." The blind person is not introduced to the dog immediately, however. First the blind person works with one of the instructors or trainers to become familiar with all of the commands the dog knows and to learn how the commands should be given. The blind person goes on walks with the trainer and holds onto the handle of a harness as the only means of communication. During this time, too, the trainer appraises the blind person so that the best possible match of dog and master can be made in terms of personalities.

When the dog and the blind person meet, they begin an intimate life together. As a team now, they repeat all of the lessons each has learned, the trainer making certain they are exposed to every possible kind of condition. If the blind person has special kinds of problems at home or at work, these are simulated at the school to prepare the dog for these particular circumstances. At evening sessions, the masters are taught how to give their dogs proper care to keep them well groomed and in good health. Any special questions they may have can be answered at those times, too.

Finally the dog and the blind person are sent off to live together, each now understanding and appreciating the other's needs. A working life of ten years can be expected for most guide dogs—some more, some less. But once a blind person has

**A "hearing" dog
responds to a door knock.**

been conditioned to depend on a dog, a loss will be replaced with another dog as quickly as possible. Requests for replacements are given top priority so that the daily life and routine of the blind person is disrupted only briefly.

"EARS" FOR THE DEAF

Some of the same schools that train dogs for the blind have in recent years been experimenting with using dogs to aid the deaf. A number of graduates from these training schools are now at work for their masters, and more are in training. As the schools learn more about the needs of deaf people and how the dogs can become helpful in solving their problems, more dogs will be put to work. They let their masters know when the telephone rings, when someone is at the door, and in similar ways become the deaf person's incredibly acute hearing aids.

The schools are also training dogs to help people who are bedridden, in wheelchairs, or paralyzed. They pick up dropped objects, get clothes, shoes, or other wearing apparel, "fetch" newspapers, mail, and similar items—and become the hands and legs of those who cannot do for themselves.

7
To the Rescue!

Saint Bernards, the kindly giants of the Alps, have been rescuing people since the early 1600s. Countless thousands have been saved by these big dogs.

The most famous was a dog named Barry who worked the snowy peaks and passes between 1800 and 1810. During those years, Barry was credited with saving forty-two people from sure death. Barry himself died of old age.

Rescue work seems almost to be a basic part of the Saint Bernard's character. Their sense of smell for finding people is uncanny, for they can locate them, dead or alive, buried many feet under the snow. They also have an unusual ability to sense when a dreaded avalanche, or White Death, is likely to come charging down a slope.

In addition to their rescue work, Saint Bernards also serve as guide dogs. They find and follow trails, and by leading the

way, they test to see if the trail will hold the people following them. A Saint Bernard is as big as a man, for it weighs from 160 to as much as 200 pounds (73 to 91 kg). On its hind legs, it may stand 6 feet (1.8 m) tall.

Nearly all Saint Bernards are gentle, and they make good pets, although they are much too large for most people to accommodate. An occasional Saint Bernard has a bad disposition, and because it is so large, it can indeed be dangerous.

The earliest of the Saint Bernards were not as large as those today. Their ancestry is closely tied to the mastiffs, with later crossbreedings with such other giants as the Great Pyrenees, Great Dane, and probably also Newfoundlands. The monks bred the dogs to achieve better rescue performance and were little concerned about looks. The dogs got their present name in the mid-1800s from the Saint Bernard Hospice high in the Alps.

TEAMWORK

Originally the Saint Bernards were trained to work in packs of four. When they found a victim, two of the dogs lay down beside the person, one on each side, to warm the body, and they licked the person's face. The other two raced back to the monastery to bring help.

Today the dogs are generally accompanied on their mercy missions by monks from the alpine hospices. The dogs do not carry casks of brandy around their necks as depicted in the famous painting by Sir Edwin Landseer.

Saint Bernard

(45)

8
Dogs on Duty

From his patrol car, Sergeant Bill Nelson saw a man rush from behind a woman walking across a park. The man grabbed the woman's shopping bag and purse, then sped off.

On foot, there was no way Sergeant Nelson could overtake and capture the purse snatcher, and to get to the other side of the park in his patrol car meant a circling drive of several blocks. The man would disappear before he got there. But the instant he saw what happened, Sergeant Nelson pressed a special button installed on the dash of his car. The door on the parked side of the patrol car whipped open.

Two other eyes had watched the purse-snatching episode, too. As the door swung open, Sergeant Nelson gave a command that sent Sundance, his German shepherd companion, speeding across the park. At 35 to 40 miles per hour (56 to 64 km per hour), more than twice as fast as the thief could run, Sundance soon caught up with the fleeing criminal. By the time Sergeant

Nelson arrived, the big dog had downed the thief and was standing over him.

Sundance did not bite, but his snarls and flashing white teeth made it obvious that he would sink his fangs bone deep if the man made a move. The purse snatcher pleaded with Sergeant Nelson to call off the vicious dog.

Vicious? Yes—but only on command. At home with Sergeant Nelson's wife and children, Sundance was docile and as playful as a pup. His dual personality was the result of his rigid training for police work, and at this moment, he was on duty.

Sundance is one of more than a dozen dogs working for the city of Miami's police department. Their pay consists of food and upkeep, plus a comfortable home. Most important to the dogs is the love and appreciation that they get from their handler. In money they cost only about 5 percent as much as a young police officer. An exact comparison is not possible, of course. Dogs cannot by any means do what a human can—but neither can a human match a dog's accomplishments. Each is well trained to utilize his or her special capabilities. Together they make a superlative team.

A dog, for example, has an exceptionally keen sense of smell—a thousand or more times better than a human's. Turned loose in a building, a dog can make a swift, thorough, and accurate search to locate anyone who might be in hiding. Within two hours, a dog can do as much work as six men in an entire day— and with less chance of error.

DEATH IN THE LINE OF DUTY

Two veteran Miami dogs died on precisely that kind of mission a few years ago. On a search detail for three armed men who

**Miami police work
with one of their dogs.**

had robbed a church, both dogs died of heat stroke in the humid 90° F (32° C) weather. They had overdone themselves in their determination to perform the duty assigned them. At the funeral for the dogs, their officer handlers wept unashamedly, for very close friends and beloved members of their families were gone.

The officers blamed themselves for having subjected the dogs to such difficult work without giving them a rest. True, the men had asked too much of the dogs, but it was unintentional. They were pushing the dogs only as they push themselves to the limit of endurance in such demanding circumstances. Neither officer had any notion that his dog was exceeding its tolerance, for both dogs were vigorous and anxious to work, showing no great evidence of tiredness.

Whatever the dogs are asked to do, they perform to the very best of their ability. If they fail, it is generally traceable to a mistake of the handler in asking them to do the impossible. When Sergeant Nelson saw the thief rob the woman in the park, Sundance made the same observation. In the patrol car, Sergeant Nelson and his dog were at the same level for vision. Out of the car, Sergeant Nelson would have towered over Sundance. All sorts of obstructions might have blocked from Sundance what Sergeant Nelson could see clearly. A handler must be aware of such circumstances and take them into account before giving the dog a command.

A LONG HISTORY
OF POLICE WORK

People charged with bringing criminals to justice have used dogs as aids for centuries. Bloodhounds have long been employed to track down fugitives and to help find people who are lost.

(49)

In June 1977, as a recent example, Sandy and Little Red tracked down James Earl Ray, the convicted killer of Martin Luther King, Jr. Ray had escaped from a prison in Tennessee and was hiding in the hills. Mastiffs and other large dogs long ago served as sentries. But it was not until the late 1800s that actual schools for training dogs in police work were established—first in Belgium, then in Germany, Italy, and other European countries.

Americans soon put dogs on duty, too. More than fifty cities in the United States now have dogs in service. These are trained dogs, much like Sundance in the city of Miami's police department. In many other police departments, dogs accompany police on their routine tours but are not specifically trained for their work.

SELECTING THE DOGS

Most of the trained dogs are put through training modeled after that used by London's Scotland Yard. Labrador retrievers, Rottweilers, poodles, and other breeds have been trained, but German shepherds predominate in police work because of their high intelligence, size, and imposing appearance.

In Miami, as nearly everywhere, the dogs are donated, relinquished by their original owners because they are no longer able to keep them where they live or because the dogs have become uncontrollable or some similar reason. Not all dogs are acceptable, of course. First they are tested for their physical condition as well as their responsiveness to training. From as many as a hundred offers, perhaps only a dozen are selected to start training, and only about half of these will complete the course. Those rejected are returned to their owners. Some dogs may not have all of the qualifications for police duty but still

**"Little Red" and "Sandy," bloodhounds
used to track down James Earl Ray
in his 1977 escape attempt.**

do well enough to serve as guards or sentries at prisons or in other confined areas.

TRAINING

A dog selected for training is immediately assigned to the officer who will become its handler. These officers have also been subjected to a careful screening. They must have a love for animals, for their dogs will be with them twenty-four hours a day. Preferably, they are family members with children. This will give the dog a good home atmosphere and an opportunity to be loved as a pet when not on duty. The handler will have full responsibility, too, for the dog's health, and the dog must be kept well groomed and properly fed.

Training for the dog and the handler lasts for three months. It begins with simple obedience training in which the dog learns to obey such commands as Sit, Down, Stay, No, Heel, Leave, Up, Fetch, and Out. Each word command also has a special hand signal so the dog learns to respond to the handler's wishes even when the voice cannot be heard.

The attention span of the very best of the dogs is brief, and so when a dog fails to respond properly, it is useless to continue with the same command over and over. The dog becomes bored and disinterested. The trainer then goes back to a command the dog has already learned and gives the dog great praise when performing as expected. Finally the dog is programmed to respond quickly and accurately when command words and signals are given.

Next the dog is taught to track. The officers take turns laying trails for each other's dogs to follow. On the softly spoken command word "Seek!" the dog will begin to follow the trail, the handler following. The dog is on a leash 25 feet (7.6 m) long when tracking. If the dog finds anything along the way that carries the scent of the suspect and was presumably dropped, this is pointed out to the handler. At first the trails are short, but by the time the dog is ready for graduation, a trail as much as a mile long and an hour old can be followed.

In the next stage, the dog learns to attack. This is the action it must take when the tracking leads finally to the suspect. If the suspect stops—and most do—when the dog moves in, then the dog simply holds the suspect at bay and barks until the handler arrives.

But if the suspect tries to run away, the dog will attack, grabbing whichever arm holds a weapon and holding it firmly until the police officer arrives. The dog is trained not to be vicious in the attacks, but neither will it let loose until given the command of Leave! But if the police officer follows that command with Watch Him!, the dog continues to hold the suspect at bay. If the suspect attempts to escape, the command of Stop Him! brings on the attack again.

In the final stage of their training, the dogs learn how to search buildings, woods, or other places where suspects may hide. In a building, the dog moves from room to room and then from one floor to the next. The dog misses no cranny, its nose unerring. In this phase of the training program, the dog also learns how to scale walls 12 feet (3.5 m) high or higher and must also be able to walk planks 6 inches (15 cm) wide to span spaces as from one building to another.

Police departments now accept dogs as one of their important "tools," in the same category as lie-detector tests and similar intruments used to achieve justice.

SIMILAR KINDS OF DUTY

Dogs are not infallible, but when performing within the framework of their capabilities, they work like machines to achieve their purpose. They can sniff out caches of drugs for narcotics agents, locate bombs or mines for the military, search for and find illegal immigrants—and continue in their off hours to be lovable dogs. A dog on duty is programmed to serve its master's particular needs. It does the job automatically and with an intensity difficult for a human to comprehend. No other animals that serve humans are more exemplary than dogs on duty.

Above, "Roland," a dachshund, has been trained to sniff out drugs. Below, "Nitro" has been trained to find explosives by smell.

(55)

9
From Pulling Carts to Outer Space

In times past, dogs pulled carts, which they still do to a limited degree in some countries today. The American Indians, who had no horses until the Europeans brought them to America, used their yellow mongrel dogs to pull travois, a triangle of poles dragged along the ground with its load slung in the space between the poles. In some countries, dogs were used also to pull farm implements.

Many dogs pulled carts in Europe, especially in Belgium, Holland, and Switzerland. For hauling light loads relatively short distances, the dogs were excellent. Their cargo was generally milk, flowers, fruits and vegetables, meat, or bakery goods. But sometimes they were made to haul coal and other heavy loads. Animal lovers became greatly concerned about this abuse and had regulations passed to limit the work demanded of these willing animals.

Rottweilers, Great Danes and most of the larger breeds have had their turn in pulling carts or hauling loads on their backs. In Belgium and Holland, the dogs most commonly used were called Leonbergers. They are believed to be crosses of Saint Bernards and Newfoundlands. In Switzerland, work dogs were Swiss mountain dogs, of which there were several types. All of the draft dogs could be traced to a mastiff ancestry.

PIONEERING THE PAST AND THE FUTURE

Since the beginning of their fast friendship with human beings, dogs have gone with people on pioneering or exploratory missions, generally working as guides, guards, or pack animals and always as good and trusted friends.

It was dogs, not people, who made the first journeys into outer space. Laika, sent into space by the Russians on Sputnik II in 1957, was the first animal to orbit the earth. The Russians did not provide for bringing her back to earth. After a week of travel in space, Laika died aboard her craft, but she had provided by a remote monitoring system much important data to pave the way for the invasion of space by humans.

Laika was followed about three years later by Pchelka and Muska. They made a two-day orbit but died when their ship burned on its way through the atmosphere back to earth. Soon afterward the Russians sent up Belka and Strelka aboard Sputnik V. These dogs made eighteen complete orbits and returned to earth safely. A puppy, called Pushinka, born to Strelka was presented by Premier Nikita Khrushchev to President John F. Kennedy to be a pet for Caroline, his daughter.

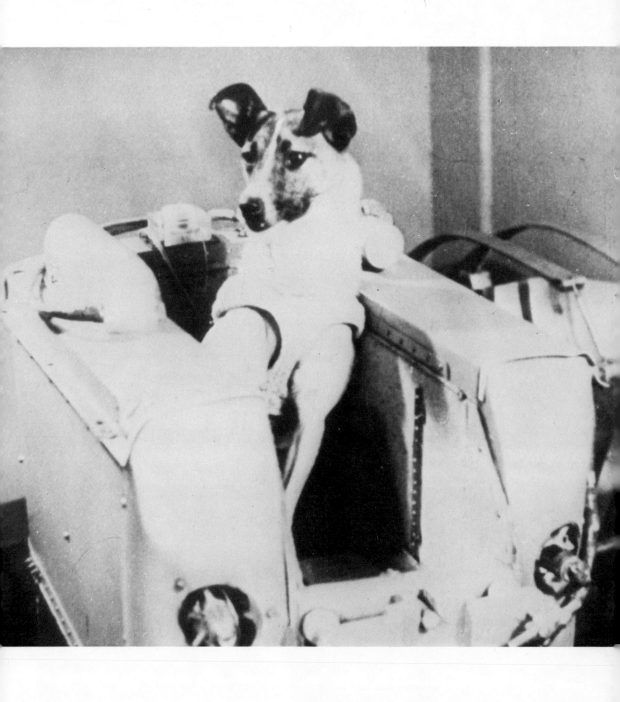

Two more dogs, Chernushka and Zvezdochka, were also put into orbit by the Russians, each dog on a separate flight, and were returned to earth successfully. The Russians then decided that the dogs had completed their work of confirming that space travel could be survived by people.

Whatever the need or mission, there is either a dog trained for the task or one willing to perform.

"Laika," aboard Sputnik II
prior to launch.

Suggested Reading

BOOKS ABOUT WORKING DOGS

Anderson, La Vere. *Balto—Sled Dog of Alaska*. Champagne, Ill.: Garrard, 1976.

Anderson, Marlene and Joan M. Brearly. *This Is the St. Bernard*. Neptune, N.J.: TFH Publications, 1973.

Baur, John E. *Dogs on the Frontier*. San Antonio: Naylor, 1964.

Bishop, Ada. *All About the Collie*. New York: British Book Center, 1971.

Brearly, Joan M. *This Is the Samoyed*. Neptune, N.J.: TFH Publications, 1975.

———. *This Is the Siberian Husky*. Neptune, N.J.: TFH Publications, 1974.

Goldbecker, William and E. Hart. *This Is the German Shepherd*. Neptune, N.J.: TFH Publications, 1964.

Handel, Leo H. *Dog Named Duke: True Stories of German Shepherds at Work with the Law*. Philadelphia: Lippincott, 1966.

Kay, Helen. *Man and Mastiff: The Story of the St. Bernard Through History*. New York: Macmillan, 1967.

Lister-Kaye, Charles. *Welsh Corgi*. New York: Arco, 1970.

GENERAL BOOKS—
WORKING DOGS AND OTHERS

Book of the Dog. London, New York: Hamlyn, 1970.

Complete Dog Book (Official Publication of the American Kennel Club). New York: Howell Book House, 1976.

Howell, Elsworth S. and Stanley Dangerfield, eds. *The International Encyclopedia of the Dog.* New York: Howell, 1971.

Jones, Arthur F. and Feredith Hamilton, eds. *The World Encyclopedia of Dogs.* New York: Galahad Books, 1971.

Man's Best Friend. Washington: National Geographic Society, 1974 (revised edition of *The Book of Dogs*).

Pugnetti, Gino. *The Great Book of Dogs.* New York: Galahad Books, 1973.

Sabin, Francene and Louis. *Dogs of America.* New York: G. P. Putnam's Sons, 1967.

Index